Fully Reproducible Copymasters

130+ Merit Certificates

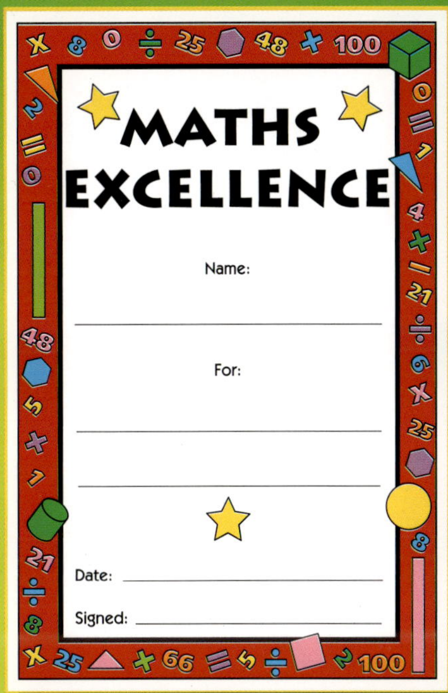

Leanne McNally

PR–0388
ISBN 1-86400-718-4
9 781864 007183

Prim-Ed Publishing
www.prim-ed.com

Merit Certificates – Primary
Prim-Ed Publishing

Published in 2002 by R.I.C. Publications
Reprinted under license in 2002 by Prim-Ed Publishing

ISBN 1 86400 718 4
PR–0388

Home Page: http://www.prim-ed.com

Prim-Ed Publishing Pty Ltd
Offices in: United Kingdom: PO Box 2840, Coventry, CV6 5ZY **Email:** sales@prim-ed.com
Australia: PO Box 332, Greenwood, Western Australia, 6924 **Email:** mail@ricgroup.com.au
Republic of Ireland: Bosheen, New Ross, County Wexford, Ireland **Email:** sales@prim-ed.com

Katie Budge

Primary

130+ Merit Certificates

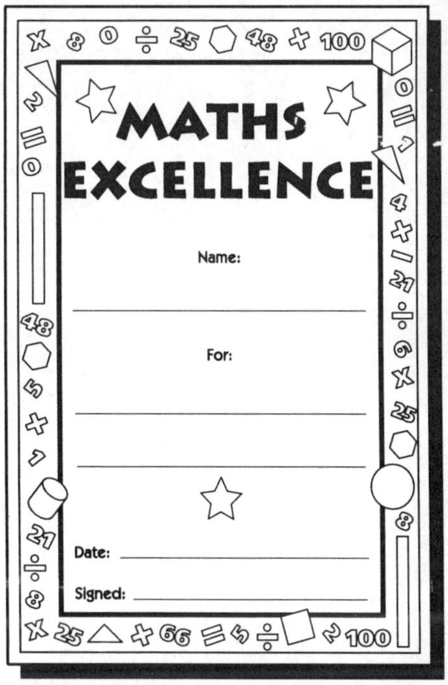

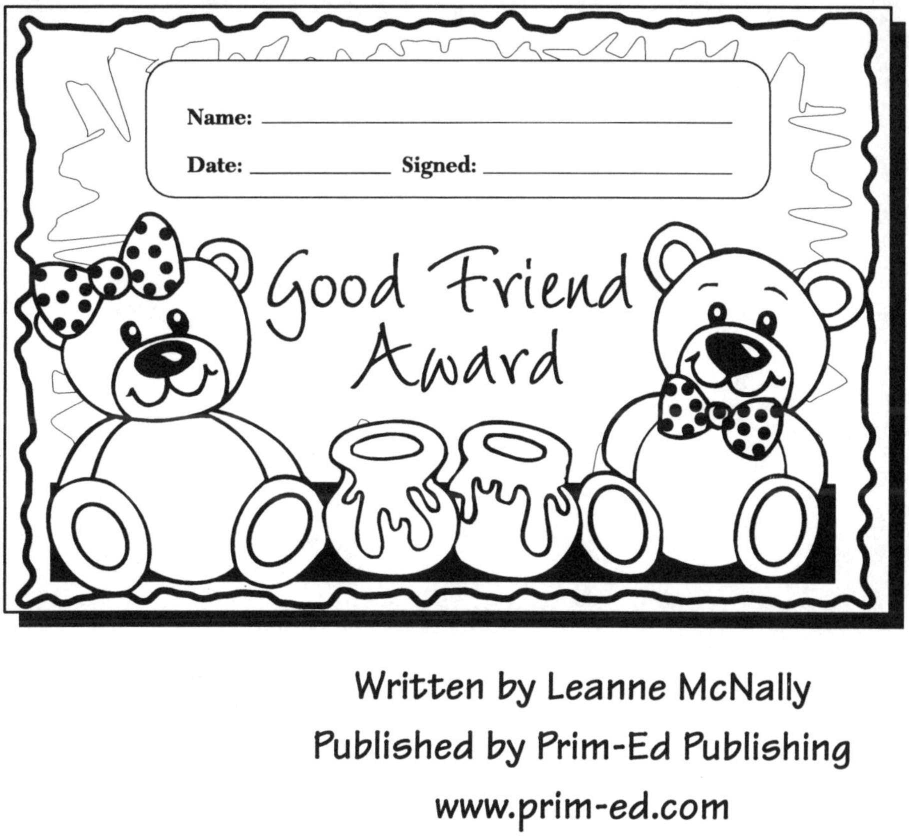

Written by Leanne McNally

Published by Prim-Ed Publishing

www.prim-ed.com

0388C

Foreword

Merit Certificates is a range of reproducible merit cards designed to encourage pupils to try their best in whatever endeavours they undertake: academic, sporting or creative.

Regular use of awards promotes self-esteem and provides a positive working environment for pupils. It is useful to keep a tally of the pupils who have received merit certificates, to ensure they all have a chance to experience increased self-esteem. (A record sheet/checklist has been included on p. ii.) Parents, too, love to see their child's efforts being acknowledged.

Each copymaster is designed to be photocopied onto coloured card, and be ready for immediate use. Cards can be individually cut and placed in a file or box, to be filled in when required. Alternatively, certificates can be photocopied onto white card and coloured by the teacher or pupil.

Many subject areas are covered by *Merit Certificates*, including English, mathematics, science, art, physical education, music and computer studies. Other certificates cover birthdays, listening skills, work habits, pupils' attitudes and behaviour and environmental responsibility.

Contents

Pupil's Name	Date	Merit Certificate Issued

Signed:

Date:

A Wizard at Reading

Name:

You wrote an 'Egg-citing' story!

Name:

Signed:

Date:

You're Such a Bookworm!

Name:

Date:

Signed:

For Having a Go at

Name:

Date:

Signed:

Name: ____________________

Date: ____________________

Signed: ____________________

Star Reader!

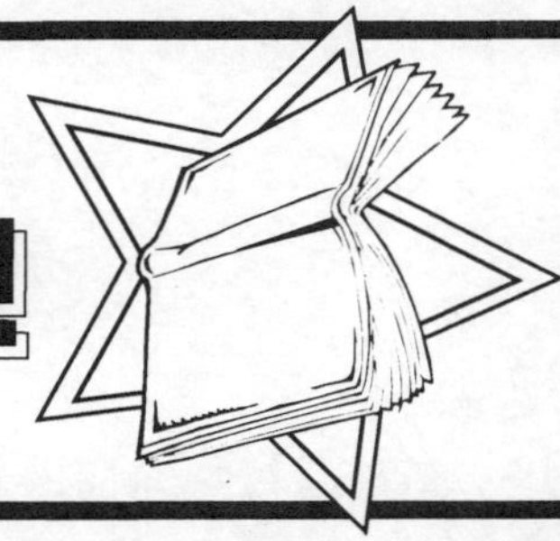

You Wrote a Fabulous Story!

Name: ____________________

Date: ____________________

Signed: ____________________

Name: ____________________

Date: ____________________

Signed: ____________________

For Achieving Your

Pen Licence

FANTASTIC HOME READING

Name: ____________________

Date: ____________________

Signed: ____________________

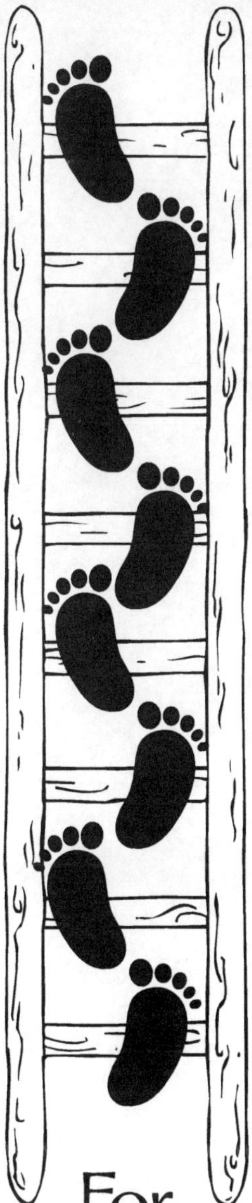

For Climbing the 'Quota' Ladder to ☐ !

Name:

Date:

Signed:

Name:

Readaholic

Date:

Signed:

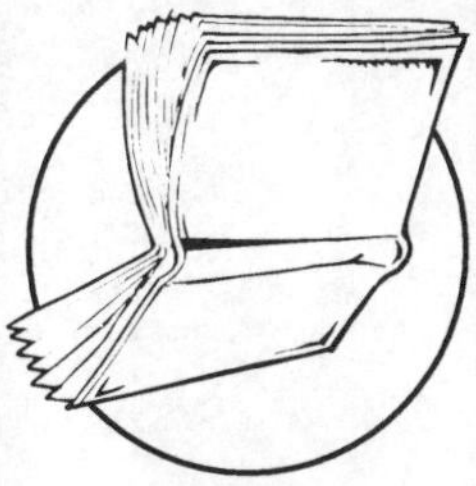

Rad Reader!

Name:

Date:

Signed:

Problem Solver

Name: ______________________

Date: __________ Signed: ______________

MATHS EXCELLENCE

Name:

____

For:

____

____

☆

Date: ______________________

Signed: ______________________

---

1 2 3 4 5 6 7 8 9 10 11 12 13 14 15 16 17 18 19 20

I Can Count to

Name:

____

Date: ______________________

Signed: ______________________

1 2 3 4 5 6 7 8 9 10 11 12 13 14 15 16 17 18 19 20

______________________ is a

MATHS WHIZ!

For: ______________________

Date: ______________________

Signed: ______________________

Great Work

You know your

___ times table

Name: ______________________

Date: ______________________

Signed: ______________________

Fantastic!

You know your

______ times table!

Name: ______________________

Date: __________ Signed: ______________

Great Computer Skills

Name:

____

Signed: ______________ **Date:** __________

Terrific Presentation when Using the Computer ...

Name: ______________________

Date: ______________________

Signed: ______________________

NATURE LOVER

' Thank you for Caring for Our Environment'

Name: ____________________

Date: ____________ Signed: ____________

Recycling Award

Congratulations

Signed: ____________

Date: ____________

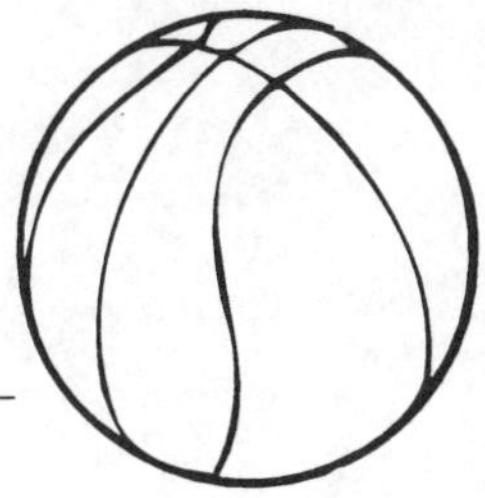

Awarded to...

____

For Being an All-round Sportsperson

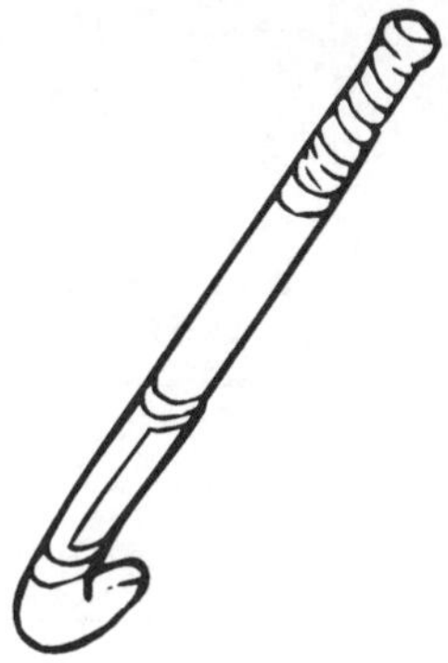

Date: ______________________________

Signed: ______________________________

You're a Winner in Every Way!

Name:

____

Date: ____________

Signed: ____________________

A Ball Sports 'All-rounder'

Name: ______________________________

Date: ______________________________

Signed: ______________________________

Jumping Ahead
By Leaps and Bounds

Name: ____________

Date: ____________ Signed: ____________

What a Legend!

You give your best to the sport you're playing!

Name: ____________

Date: ____________ Signed: ____________

A 'Run'away Success!

Name:

____

For Being Such a Terrific Runner

Date: ____________ Signed: ____________

Player of the Day

Name: ____________

Date: ____________

Signed: ____________

For Taking Part in the Race

EVENT: ____________________

Name: ____________________

Date: ____________________

Signed: ____________________

Fantastic Swim

WELL DONE!

Name:

Event: ____________________

Place: ____________________

Date: __________ Signed: __________

Super Effort!!

Name: ____________________

Date: __________ **Signed:** __________

For Being on the 'Ball' ...

and Following Instructions!

Date: __________ **Signed:** __________

Name: ____________________

You Sing Like a Bird

Name: ____________________

Date: ____________________

Signed: ____________________

Art Award!

Name: ____________________

Signed: ____________________

Date: ____________________

Genius at Work!

Name: ____________________

Date: ____________________

Signed: ____________________

Great Performance

Name:

____

Signed: ____________ Date: ____________

It Sounds Like You've Tried Your Best

Name:

Date:

Signed:

A Musical Genius

Name:

Date: Signed:

Player of the Day

Name:

Date: Signed:

A Noteworthy Performance

Name:

Date: *Signed:*

You've had such a 'buzzy' day!!
Name:
Date:
Signed:

For not giving up
Name:
Date:
Signed:

For always being cheerful
Name:
Date:
Signed:

You are so handy to have around!
Thank You for Helping
Name:
Date:
Signed:

You always look on the bright side!

Name: ____________________

Date: __________ Signed: ____________________

Well Done!!

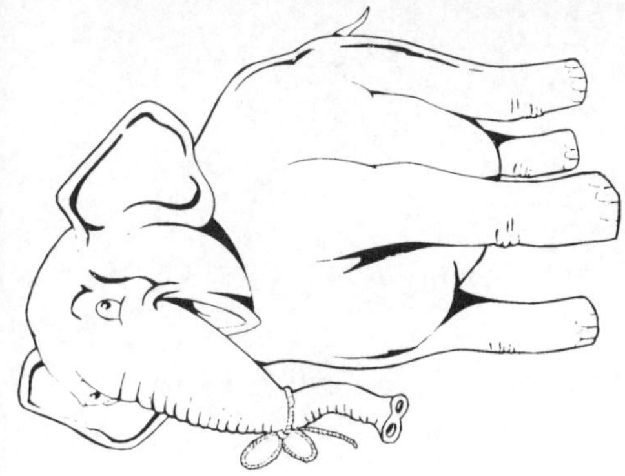

You remembered to bring... ____________________

Name: ____________________

Date: __________ Signed: ____________________

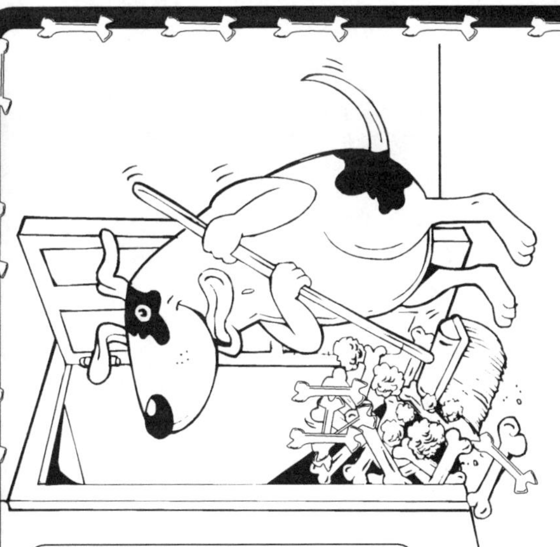

For Keeping *Your Work Area* Clean and Tidy !

Name: ____________________

Date: __________ Signed: ____________________

Congratulations for Taking the Plunge in

____

Name: ____________________

Date: __________ Signed: ____________________

Love Your Smile!

Name: ______________________

Date: ______________________

Signed: ______________________

'Best Foot Forward' Award

Name: ______________________

Date: ____________ Signed: ____________

Name: ______________________

You Tried and Succeeded at

____

Date: ____________ Signed: ____________

Name: ______________________

Congratulations

You worked nicely in your group

Date: ____________ Signed: ____________

I like the way you're trying your best in

Name: ____________________

Date: __________ Signed: __________

For Your Best Effort! in...

____

Name: ____________________

Date: ____________________

Signed: ____________________

Good Friend Award

Name: ____________________

Date: __________ Signed: __________

Name: ____________________

Date: __________ Signed: __________

Achieving Your Goal in

____

____

____

Good Friend Award

Name: ____________

Date: ____________

Signed: ____________

For Being So Caring!

Name: ____________

Date: ____________

Signed: ____________

Name:

____

Certificate of Friendship

Date: ____________ Signed: ____________

Certificate of Friendship

For Being a Great Friend!

Name: ____________

Date: ____________

Signed: ____________

Neat Work

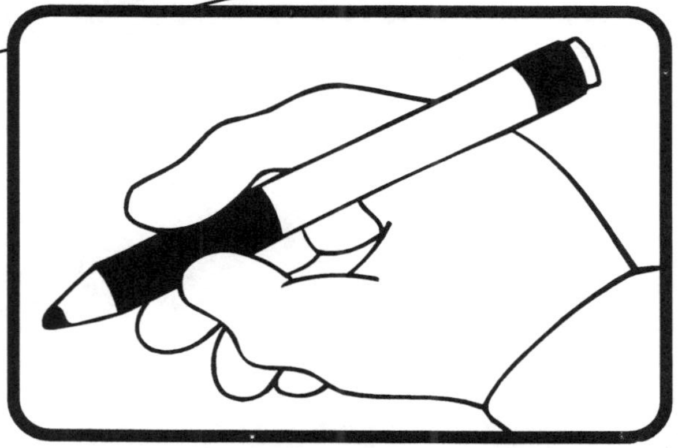

Name: ____________________

Date: __________ **Signed:** __________

Excellent Presentation

Name: ____________________

Date: ____________________

Signed: ____________________

Fantastic Presentation

Name: ____________________

Date: ____________________

Signed: ____________________

Neat Work

Name: ____________________

Date: ____________________

Signed: ____________________

Today's Best Listener!

Name: ______________________

Date: ______________________

Signed: ______________________

For Listening Well!

Name:

____

Date: ______________ **Signed:** ______________

Let's Celebrate!

You're Such a Good Listener

Name:

____

Date: ______________ Signed: ______________

You listened to my instructions carefully ...

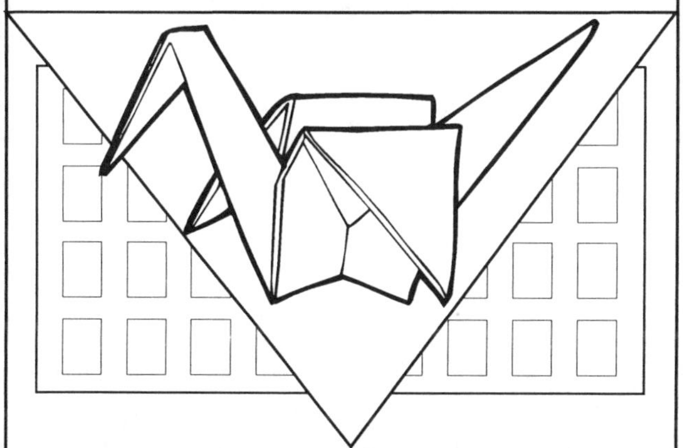

WELL DONE!

Name: ______________________

Date: ______________________

Signed: ______________________

I Loved the Way You Listened Today!

Name: ______________________

Date: ____________ **Signed:** ____________

No Clowning Around!

Fantastic Listening!!

Name: ______________________

Date: ______________________

Signed: ______________________

Terrific Listener

Name: ______________________

Date: ______________________

Signed: ______________________

Cool Cat!

Great Listening!

Name:

____

Date: Signed:

____________ ____________

Tidy Class Award

Congratulations to everyone in

____

You have shown pride in both your classroom and your school, by keeping them clean and tidy. Well done!!

Date: ______________________ *Signed:* ______________________

Congratulations!

What a Fantastic Class

For: ______________________ Date: ______________________

Class: ______________________ Signed: ______________________

Principal's Award

Congratulations

Name: ____________________

Date: ____________________

Signed: ____________________

Head Teacher's Award

Congratulations

Name: ____________________

Date: ____________________

Signed: ____________________

Top Job Award

Congratulations!

For doing such a top job!

Signed: ______________________

Date: ______________________

EXTRA! EXTRA!

Read all about it!!

Name: ______________________

has achieved: ______________________

____

____

____

____

____

Date: __________ **Signed:** ______________________

Bright Spark!

Name: ____________

Date: ____________

Signed: ____________

Make Tracks To Your Library

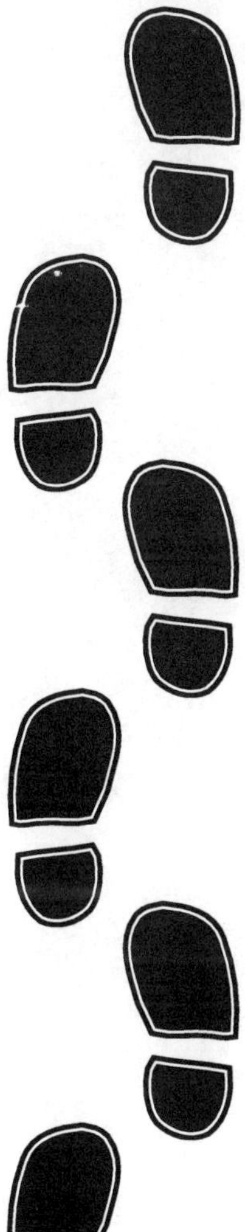

Name: ____________

Date: ____________

Signed: ____________

I can do this, standing on one hand!

Name: ____________

Date: ____________

Signed: ____________

Congratulations

Your Work

in

Is a Winner!

Signed: ____________ Date: ____________

LIBRARY AWARD

Congratulations!

For using the library and looking after the books

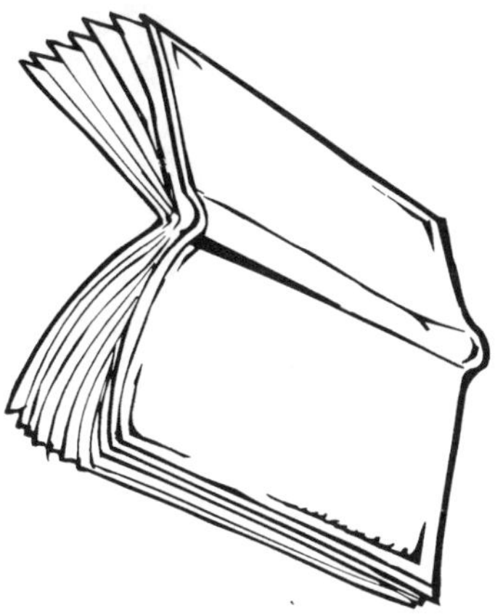

Date: ____________

Signed: ____________

Happy Birthday to You!

From all your classmates in

____

Date: ____________________

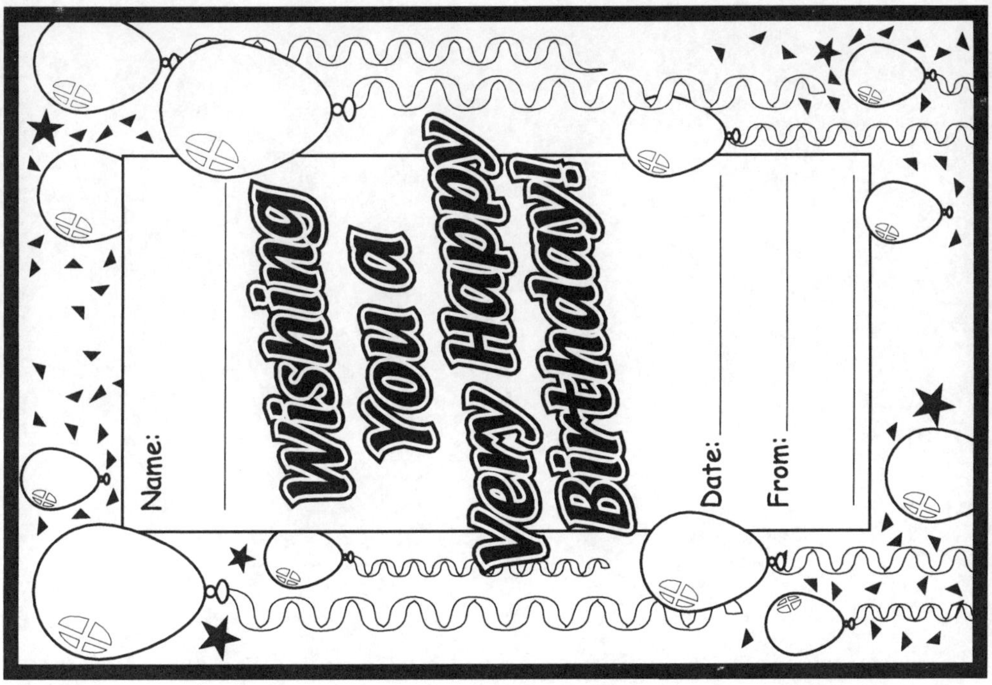
Wishing you a very Happy Birthday!
Name:
Date:
From:

STAR OF THE DAY
For:
Name:
Date:
Signed:

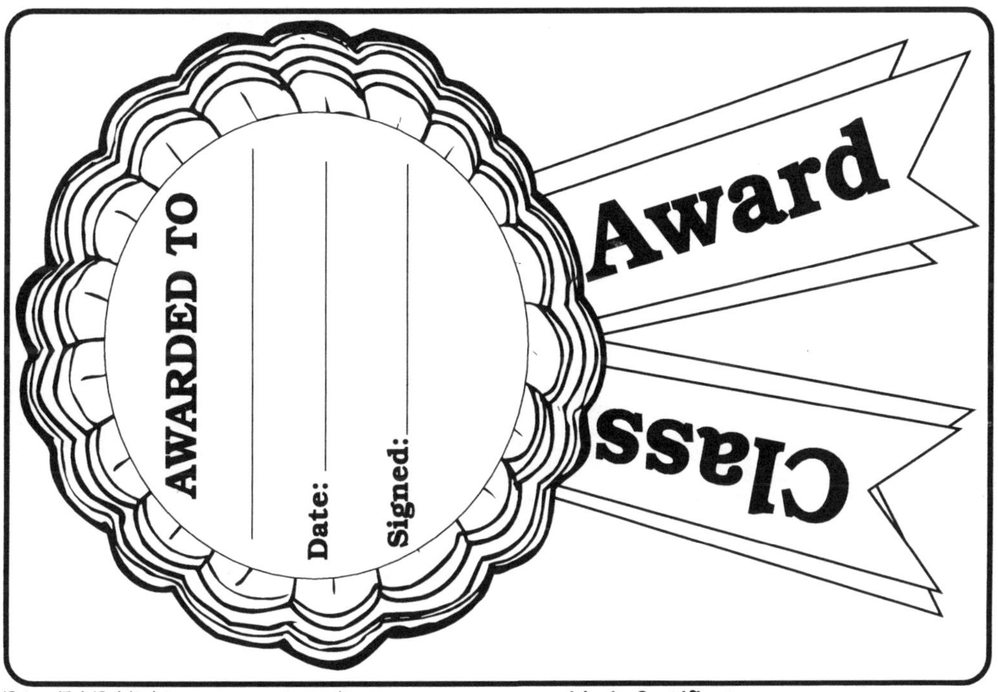
AWARDED TO
Date:
Signed:
Award
Class

PARTY
Happy Birthday
Name:
Date:
Signed:

You're Getting Along Swimmingly in.....

____

Name: ______________________

Date: ______________________

Signed: ____________________

Flying High

IN: ______________________

Name: ______________________

Date: ______________________

Signed: ____________________

You caught on quickly!

In: ______________________

Name: ______________________

Date: ____________ Signed: ____________

Fantastic Effort

Date:

____

Signed:

____

Name:

____

Wicked!

Well Done

For: ____________________

____

Name: ____________________

Date: __________ **Signed:** __________

For Such a Great Effort!

____

____

Name: ____________________

Signed: ____________________

Date: ____________________

Name: ____________________

Date: ____________________

Signed: ____________________

SO COOL!!

Sailing Through!

Name: ____________________

Date: ____________________

Signed: ____________________

Go For It!

Name: ____________

Date: ____________

Signed: ____________

Congratulations on Your Success

in

____

Name: ____________

Date: ____________ Signed: ____________

TOP ACHIEVEMENT AWARD

Name: ____________

Date: ____________

Signed: ____________

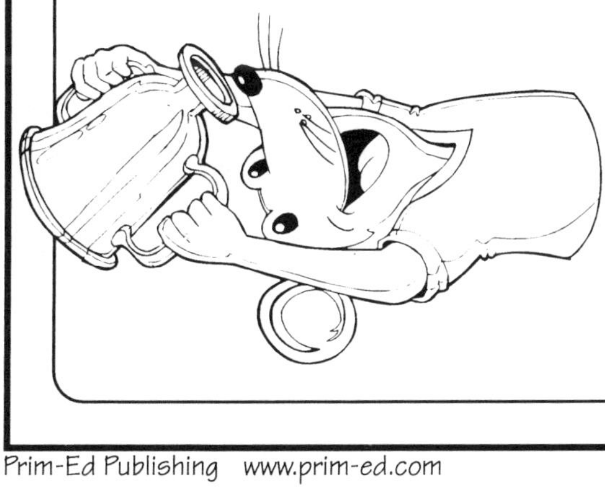

in: ____________

Genius at Work!

Name: ____________

Date: ____________

Signed: ____________

COOL WORK

NAME: ______________

DATE: ______________

SIGNED: ______________

OUT OF THIS WORLD!

Name: ______________

Date: ______________

Signed: ______________

You are 'Beary' Clever!

Name: ______________

Date: ______________

Signed: ______________

Congratulations on making it to the

TOP!

in

____

Name: ______________

Signed: ______________

Date: ______________

What a 'Genie'-us

Name: ______________________

Signed: ______________ Date: ______________

Magic Effort

For: ______________________

____

Name: ______________________

Signed: ______________ Date: ______________

Super Speller!

Name:

____

Date: ______________ Signed: ______________

Name: ______________________

For: ______________________

Date: ______________ ***Signed:*** ______________

You're Very Clever!

Speeding RIGHT ALONG!

Name:

Date:

Signed:

You Are Sooooo Clever!

Name:

Date:

Signed:

You're a **Team** Player!

Name:

Date: Signed:

Your work is always magic!

Name:

Date:

Signed:

WAY TO GO!

Name: ______________________

For: ______________________

____

____

Date: ______________________

Signed: ______________________

Good Work

Name: ______________________

Date: ______________________

Signed: ______________________

100% Correct

IN

____

Name: ______________________

Date: ______________________

Signed: ______________________

What a Bright Spark!

Name: ______________________

Date: ____________ Signed: ______________________

Name: ____________________

Date: __________ **Signed:** ______________

Class Award

Name:

For: ______________

Signed: ______________

Date: ______________

Well Done

Name: ____________________

For: ____________________

Date: __________ **Signed:** __________

Great Try

Name: ____________________

Date: ____________________

Signed: ____________________

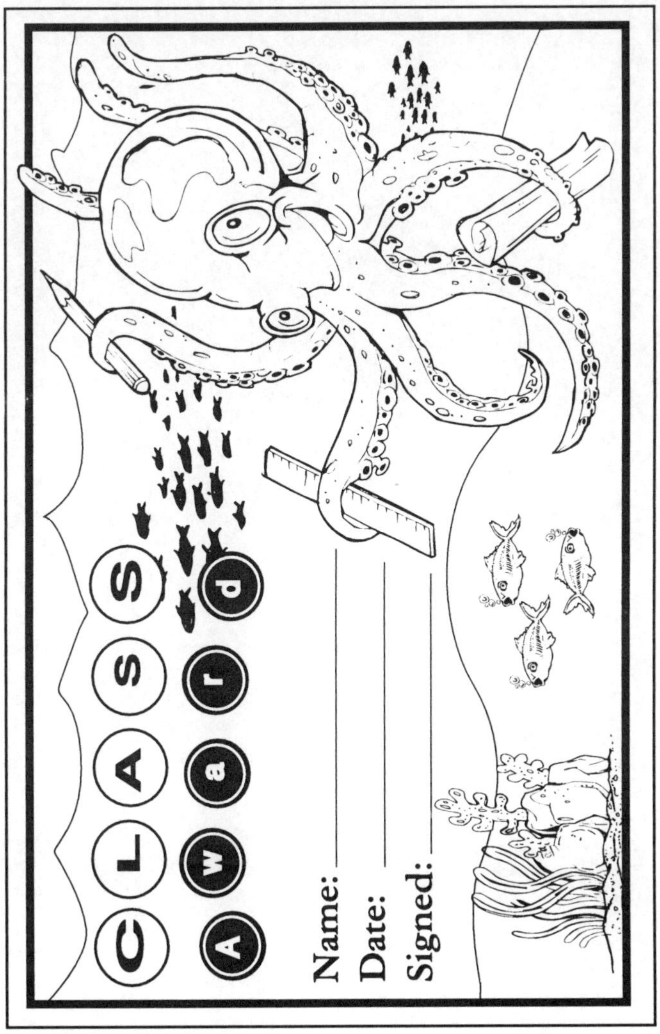
CLASS
Award
Name:
Date:
Signed:

100% Club!
For Achieving 100% in
Name:
Date:
Signed:

Name:
Date:
Signed:
Wonderful
Effort!

TERRIFIC
WORK
Name:
Date:
Signed:

THE TICK OF APPROVAL

GREAT WORK

in: ______________________

Name: ______________________

Date: ______________________

Signed: ______________________

Extra! Extra!

Read all about it!!

Name:

____

Has: ______________________

____

____

Signed: ____________ Date: ____________

Full Steam Ahead!

You're Trying Hard— Keep Going

Name: ____________ Signed: ____________

Date: ____________

Racing Ahead by Leaps and Bounds

Name: ______________________

For: ______________________

Date: ____________ *Signed:* ____________

TEACHER'S
Award
Name:
Date:
Signed:

Great Teamwork!
Name:
Date:
Signed:

Fantastic
Effort
Today!
Well Done!!!
Name:
Date:
Signed:

Star Student
Name:
Date:
Signed:

Pupil of the Day

Congratulations!

Name: ______________________

Date: ______________________

Signed: ______________________

Name: ______________________

For Staying on Task and Working Quietly

Date: ______________________

Signed: ______________________

Name: ______________________

Date: ______________________

Signed: ______________________

Marvellous Work!

Terrific Effort!

Name: ______________________

Date: ______________________

Signed: ______________________

Honour Certificate

Awarded to

____

For: ______________________________

____

Date: ____________________ Signed: ____________________